P9-CQO-947

Coding in Scratch: Games Workbook

Written by

Jon Woodcock
& Steve Setford

Written by
Jon Woodcock & Steve Setford
Editor Steve Setford
Designer Peter Radcliffe
US Editors Jenny Siklos, Allison Singer
Publisher Sarah Larter
Art Director Martin Wilson
Jacket Designers Charlotte Jennings/Emma Hobson
Producer, Pre-Production Nadine King
Producer Priscilla Reby
Publishing Director Sophie Mitchell

First American Edition, 2016
Published in the United States by DK Publishing
345 Hudson Street, New York, New York 10014

Copyright © 2016 Dorling Kindersley Limited
DK, a Division of Penguin Random House LLC
17 18 19 20 10 9 8 7 6 5 4 3 2
005–288590–January/2016

A catalog record for this book
is available from the Library of Congress.
ISBN 978-1-4654-4482-0

DK books are available at special discounts when purchased
in bulk for sales promotions, premiums, fund-raising, or
educational use. For details, contact: DK Publishing Special
Markets, 345 Hudson Street, New York, New York 10014
SpecialSales@dk.com

Printed and bound in China

Scratch is developed by the Lifelong Kindergarten group
at MIT Media Lab. See http://scratch.mit.edu

A WORLD OF IDEAS:
SEE ALL THERE IS TO KNOW

www.dk.com

Contents

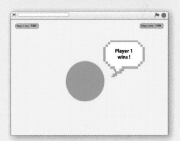
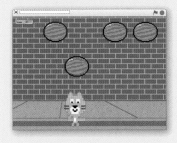

Meet Scratch

If you want to make computer games, Scratch is a great place to start. A game is a set of detailed instructions, or "program," followed by the computer. Scratch uses ready-made blocks that make building programs easy.

What you'll learn:
• Scratch is easy to learn for beginners
• You need to use **Scratch version 2.0**
• In Scratch, programs are called scripts
• What the ingredients of a Scratch project are

What's what in Scratch

In a typical Scratch project, such as a game, programs called scripts control characters and objects known as sprites. The sprites appear in a part of the Scratch screen called the stage.

The cat sprite appears whenever you start a new Scratch project

Hello!

Sprites

Sprites are things that can move around or react in a game. They can be animals and people, or even cakes and spaceships! You build scripts to bring sprites to life.

Scripts

Scripts are made of colored blocks that you drag with a computer mouse and put together like jigsaw pieces. Each block contains one instruction. Scratch reads through a script from top to bottom.

when 🏴 clicked
move (10) steps
say Hello!

Script makes cat walk 10 steps and then say "Hello!"

READ ME!

This book is based on **Scratch 2.0**, the latest version of Scratch at the time of writing. The games won't work on older versions, so make sure you have 2.0. **See page 40 for details on how to get Scratch.**

Costumes

Many sprites have two or more different pictures, or "costumes," they can show on the stage. For example, the ballerina sprite has four different costumes to "wear."

Lucky me!

The stage

All the action in a Scratch game takes place on the stage. Sprites can move around on the stage, often in front of a background image called a "backdrop." Scratch measures distances on the stage in units called steps. The stage is 480 steps wide and 360 steps tall.

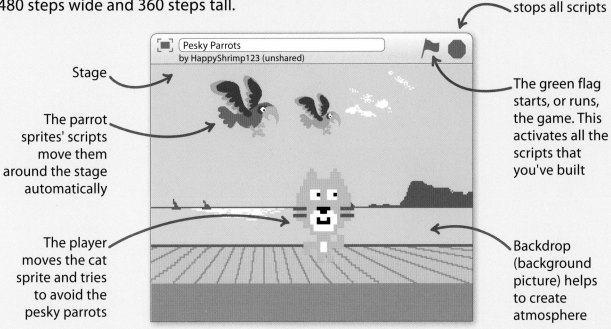

The red button stops all scripts

The green flag starts, or runs, the game. This activates all the scripts that you've built

Stage

The parrot sprites' scripts move them around the stage automatically

The player moves the cat sprite and tries to avoid the pesky parrots

Backdrop (background picture) helps to create atmosphere

Pesky Parrots
by HappyShrimp123 (unshared)

Libraries

Scratch has collections of sprites and backdrops that you can load into your projects. These collections are called libraries. There is also a library of sounds and music clips that you can use to make your games more fun.

Right-clicking

Sometimes in Scratch you need to "right click" with the computer mouse. Don't worry if you only have one button on your mouse. Instead of right-clicking, you can usually hold down the control (CTRL/ctrl) or shift key as you click.

Show what you know

Think you know the Scratch basics? Then it's time to test yourself!

1. A character or object that can move or react is a ....

2. A .... is a set of blocks joined together.

3. A .... is a picture that a sprite can show on the stage.

4. To run (start) a program, you click the ....

5. A .... is a collection of sprites, sounds, or backdrops.

6. Scratch measures distances on the stage in units called ....

Exploring Scratch

When you open Scratch, this is what you'll see. All you need to create and play games is on this screen. Take a look around and get to know Scratch.

Experiment!
• Click the buttons and tabs to experiment
• Learn what each block color does
• Try building scripts

Change language

Save projects here

Delete sprite or script

Help tool

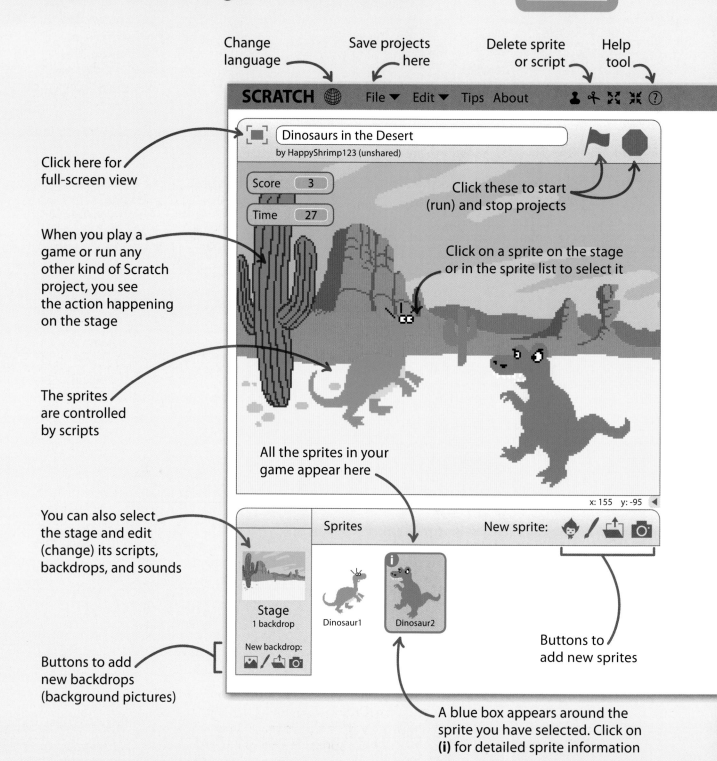

Click here for full-screen view

When you play a game or run any other kind of Scratch project, you see the action happening on the stage

The sprites are controlled by scripts

You can also select the stage and edit (change) its scripts, backdrops, and sounds

Buttons to add new backdrops (background pictures)

Click these to start (run) and stop projects

Click on a sprite on the stage or in the sprite list to select it

All the sprites in your game appear here

Buttons to add new sprites

A blue box appears around the sprite you have selected. Click on (i) for detailed sprite information

▶ Map of the Scratch editor

The stage is where projects such as games are run. The sprite list shows all the project's sprites. Script blocks can be found in the blocks palette. Build your scripts in the scripts area.

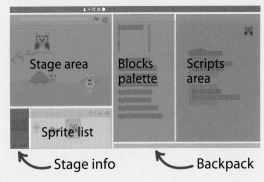

Stage area

Blocks palette

Scripts area

Sprite list

Stage info

Backpack

Costumes tab—use this to change a sprite's appearance

Sounds tab—use this to change the sounds a sprite makes

Click here for step-by-step guides and tips

Scripts tab

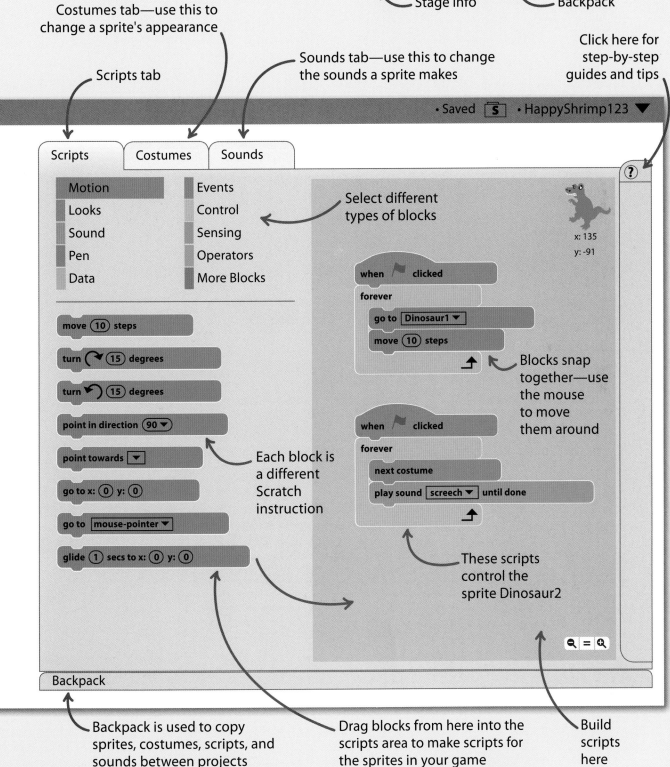

• Saved ⑤ • HappyShrimp123 ▼

Scripts   Costumes   Sounds

Motion
Looks
Sound
Pen
Data

Events
Control
Sensing
Operators
More Blocks

Select different types of blocks

x: 135
y: -91

when ⚑ clicked
forever
    go to Dinosaur1 ▼
    move 10 steps

move 10 steps

turn ↻ 15 degrees

turn ↺ 15 degrees

point in direction 90 ▼

point towards ▼

go to x: 0 y: 0

go to mouse-pointer ▼

glide 1 secs to x: 0 y: 0

Blocks snap together—use the mouse to move them around

Each block is a different Scratch instruction

when ⚑ clicked
forever
    next costume
    play sound screech ▼ until done

These scripts control the sprite Dinosaur2

🔍 = 🔍

Backpack

Backpack is used to copy sprites, costumes, scripts, and sounds between projects

Drag blocks from here into the scripts area to make scripts for the sprites in your game

Build scripts here

Fishball

Are you ready to build Fishball, your first Scratch game? Don't worry, you won't have to do it all at once. Just follow the numbered steps and put the project together piece by piece.

What you'll learn:
- How to build simple scripts to make a game
- How to add sprites, backdrops, and sounds to improve your game
- How to keep track of the time and score

The score and time left in the game are shown here

The fish follows the ball around the stage

Use the green flag and red button to start and stop the game

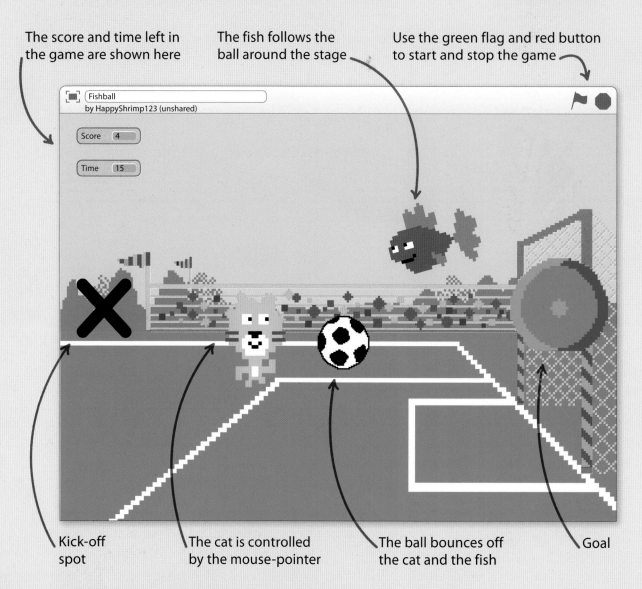

Kick-off spot

The cat is controlled by the mouse-pointer

The ball bounces off the cat and the fish

Goal

▲ Playing the game

Scratch Cat is playing soccer. Use the mouse-pointer to move him around the stage and try to deflect the ball onto the green circle to score a goal. But watch out for the fish goalkeeper—she will do her best to stop you!

Control your cat!

We'll start by creating a simple script to control the cat sprite. It will make the cat stick to the mouse-pointer like glue!

1 Open the Scratch editor: either choose **Create** on the Scratch website or click the Scratch symbol on your computer. Call the project "Fishball."

2 Under the **Scripts** tab, go to the dark blue **Motion** section of the blocks palette. Click on the **go to mouse-pointer** block and drag it to the right into the scripts area.

3 Now click the yellow **Control** section and select the **forever** block. Drag it over the **go to** block, then let go. The two blocks will lock together.

4 Next, choose the brown **Events** section of the blocks palette. Click on the **when green flag clicked** block and add it to the top of the **forever** block. Read the script through. What do you think it does?

Forever loops

Loops are sections of code that repeat again and again. A **forever** loop repeats the blocks inside it—forever! In your script to control the cat, the **forever** loop keeps the cat "glued" to the mouse-pointer for the whole game.

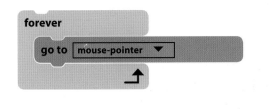

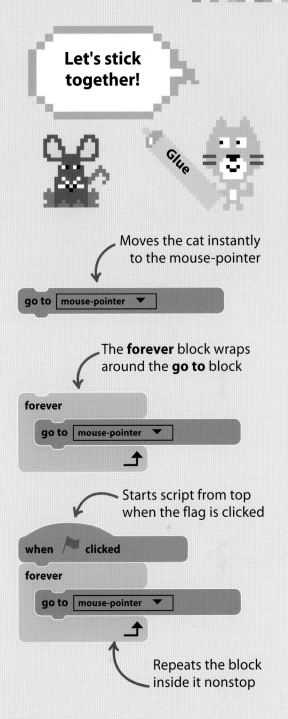

Let's stick together!

Moves the cat instantly to the mouse-pointer

`go to mouse-pointer ▼`

The **forever** block wraps around the **go to** block

`forever`
`go to mouse-pointer ▼`

Starts script from top when the flag is clicked

`when ⚑ clicked`
`forever`
`go to mouse-pointer ▼`

Repeats the block inside it nonstop

5 Click the green flag at the top of the stage to start (run) the script. The cat should move with the mouse-pointer. If not, check back through steps 1 to 4.

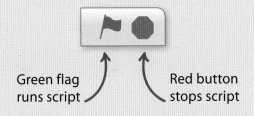

Green flag runs script

Red button stops script

Scratch Cat needs a ball

Now that you can control the cat, it's time to give him a ball to play with. You'll need to create scripts for the ball to make it bounce around the stage and off the cat.

Menus and windows

Some blocks have a "drop-down" menu, such as the **point toward** and **touching?** blocks. Click the little triangle to see the options. Then select the one you want.

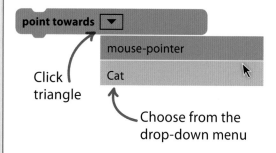

Click triangle

Choose from the drop-down menu

With other blocks, such as **turn arrow degrees**, you click in the window and type in a number.

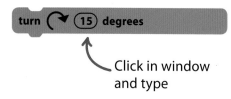

Click in window and type

if-then blocks have a pointed window into which you drag a another block that asks a question.

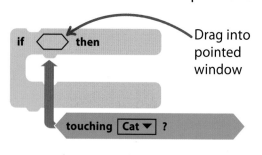

Drag into pointed window

6 Go to the sprite list and click on the **Choose sprite from library** button (the sprite symbol). In the sprite library, select "Soccer Ball" and click **OK**. The ball will appear in the sprite list.

Click the sprite symbol

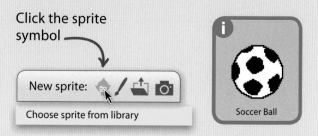

7 Next, put these blocks together in the soccer ball's scripts area. Remember that the color of a block tells you which section you can find it in on the blocks palette.

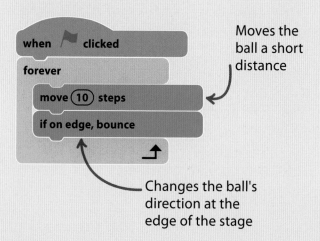

Moves the ball a short distance

Changes the ball's direction at the edge of the stage

8 Click the green flag and watch the ball bounce when it hits the edge of the stage. It won't pay any attention to the cat just yet. The green flag starts the scripts for both the ball and the cat and runs them at the same time.

I'm ignoring the cat!

9 You can make your scripts easier to understand by renaming the cat sprite. In the sprite list (below the stage), select the cat and click on the blue **(i)** in its top corner. Type "Cat" instead of "Sprite1" in the window of the sprite's information panel.

Type "Cat" in this window to change the sprite's name

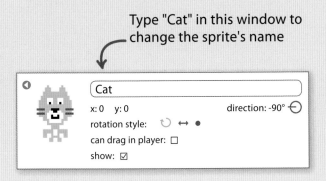

Cat

x: 0   y: 0   direction: -90°
rotation style:
can drag in player: ☐
show: ☑

if-then

An **if-then** block wraps around other blocks and uses a "true or false?" type question to control when the blocks are run. When Scratch reaches an **if-then** block, it runs the blocks inside only if the answer to the question is true.

Is the ball touching the cat?

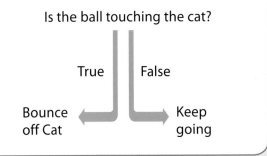

True   False

Bounce   Keep
off Cat   going

10 Now select the soccer ball sprite and put together these blocks to add to its script. Place them in the **forever** loop, after the **if on edge, bounce** block. When the ball touches the cat, the script plays a pop sound and makes the ball appear to bounce off the cat.

The **if-then** block checks to see if the ball is touching the cat

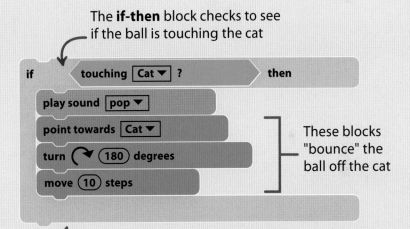

if   touching Cat ▼ ?   then

play sound pop ▼

point towards Cat ▼

turn ↻ 180 degrees

move 10 steps

These blocks "bounce" the ball off the cat

If the ball's not touching the cat, the script ignores the instructions inside the **if-then** block

when ⚑ clicked

forever

move 10 steps

if on edge, bounce

if   touching Cat ▼ ?   then

play sound pop ▼

point towards Cat ▼

turn ↻ 180 degrees

move 10 steps

11 The script for the soccer ball should now look like this. Click the green flag to test the script. The cat can now play with the ball. You should be able to move the cat around and deflect the ball by touching it. If not, check the script carefully.

Kicking off, scoring goals

Scratch Cat wants a kick-off spot and a goal to score in. A special kind of block called a variable will help you keep track of how many goals are scored during the game.

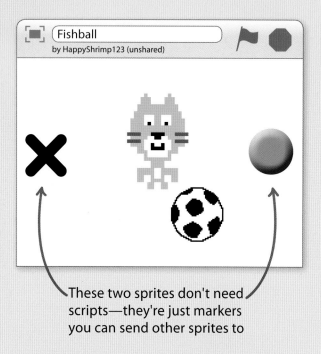

Fishball
by HappyShrimp123 (unshared)

These two sprites don't need scripts—they're just markers you can send other sprites to

Variables

A variable is like a labeled box in which you can store data, such as words or numbers. The data stored in a variable is known as its value. The new variable you made has a label, **Score**. It stores the number of goals the cat scores in a game of Fishball. The number of goals is the variable's value.

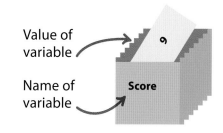

Value of variable

Name of variable

Score

12 Load two new sprites from the library: "Button1" (the green circle) and "Button5" (the black ✕). Drag Button1 to the right of the stage, halfway down, and rename it "Goal." Then drag Button5 to halfway down on the left and rename it "Start."

Sprites   New sprite:

Cat   Soccer Ball   Goal   Start

The new sprites will appear in the sprite list

13 In the orange **Data** blocks, click on **Make a Variable**. Type **"Score"** as the variable's name in the pop-up window and hit **OK**. When the block for the variable **Score** appears in the **Data** section, make sure the checkbox beside it is checked.

Type in this window

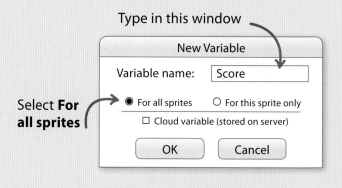

New Variable

Variable name: Score

Select **For all sprites**

● For all sprites   ○ For this sprite only
□ Cloud variable (stored on server)

OK   Cancel

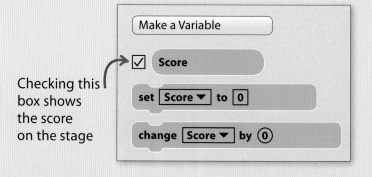

Make a Variable

☑ **Score**

set Score ▼ to 0

change Score ▼ by 0

Checking this box shows the score on the stage

14 Next, put these two blocks into the soccer ball's script after the **when green flag clicked** block and before the **forever** loop. The orange **set to** block sets the score to zero at the beginning of the game. The dark blue **go to** block sends the ball to the black ✕ ready for the kick-off.

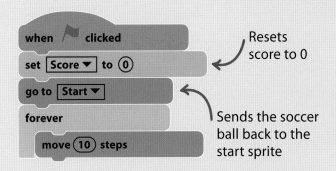

Resets score to 0

Sends the soccer ball back to the start sprite

15 You can add a sound to signal when a goal is scored. Select the soccer ball, go to the **Sounds** tab, and click on **Choose sound from library** (the speaker symbol). In the library, select "rattle" and click **OK** to load it into the project.

Sounds for the sprite can be seen under this tab

The "rattle" sound will appear under the **Sounds** tab

Click on the speaker symbol to go to the sound library

I prefer tennis!

16 Click on the **Scripts** tab and insert the group of blocks below into the ball's script. Place it under the first **if-then** group, but not inside it. Make sure it is still inside the **forever** loop. You can see the whole script in the next step.

This block, from **Sensing** section, detects when ball touches goal

Rattle sound plays each time a goal is scored

The blocks inside the **if-then** block are run only when the ball is touching the goal

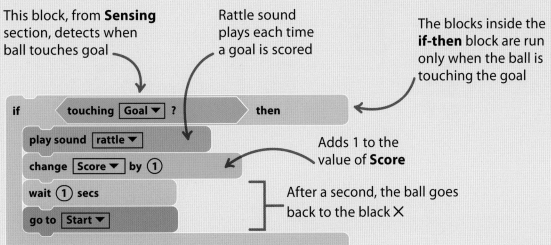

Adds 1 to the value of **Score**

After a second, the ball goes back to the black ✕

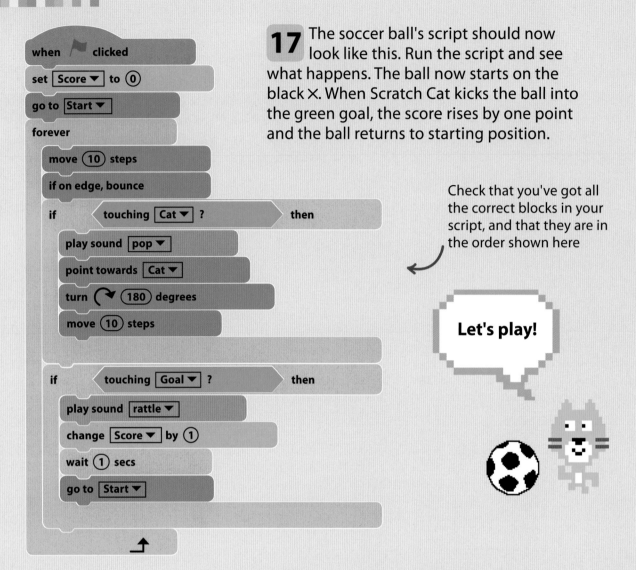

17 The soccer ball's script should now look like this. Run the script and see what happens. The ball now starts on the black ✕. When Scratch Cat kicks the ball into the green goal, the score rises by one point and the ball returns to starting position.

Check that you've got all the correct blocks in your script, and that they are in the order shown here

Let's play!

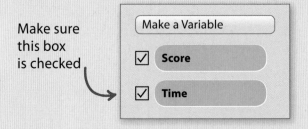

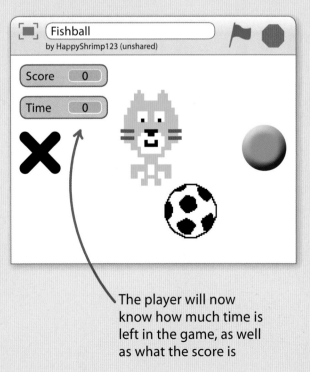

The player will now know how much time is left in the game, as well as what the score is

The pressure's on!

Games are more difficult under pressure. Adding a time limit will make Fishball more challenging. When the green flag is clicked, a 30-second countdown will start.

18 Make a new variable for all sprites called **"Time."** Leave its checkbox checked so that it shows on the stage.

Make sure this box is checked

Make a Variable
☑ **Score**
☑ **Time**

19 Add this script to the cat sprite. It will run totally separately from the other script, but at the same time.

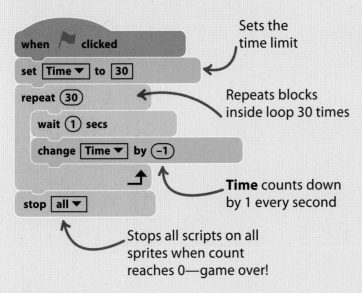

Sets the time limit

Repeats blocks inside loop 30 times

Time counts down by 1 every second

Stops all scripts on all sprites when count reaches 0—game over!

20 Try the game now. How many goals can you score in 30 seconds?

Fishy business

The game's about to get a lot harder! You're going to add a fish goalkeeper to try to stop Scratch Cat from scoring!

Fish1

21 Go to the sprite library and load "Fish1." Build the script shown on the right in the fish's scripts area. The fish should now always swim slowly toward the ball.

22 Select the soccer ball. Add this group of blocks to the ball's script to make it bounce off the fish. (It's the same as the code that makes the ball bounce off the cat, but with "Cat" changed to "Fish1" twice.) Put it *between* the two **if-then** blocks, but not inside either of them.

Repeat loops

A **repeat loop** repeats the blocks inside it only a fixed number of times, then the next blocks in the script are run. In your time-limit code, the loop takes 1 off the value of **Time** 30 times, then the action moves to the next block (**stop all**).

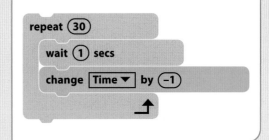

You'll never get past me!

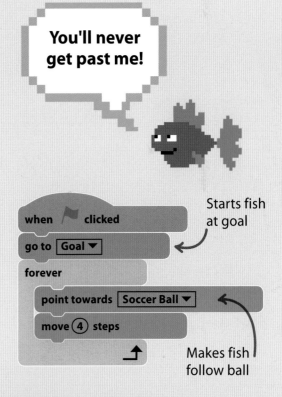

Starts fish at goal

Makes fish follow ball

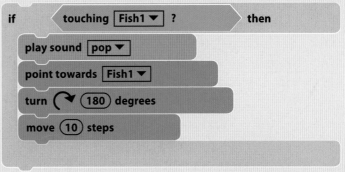

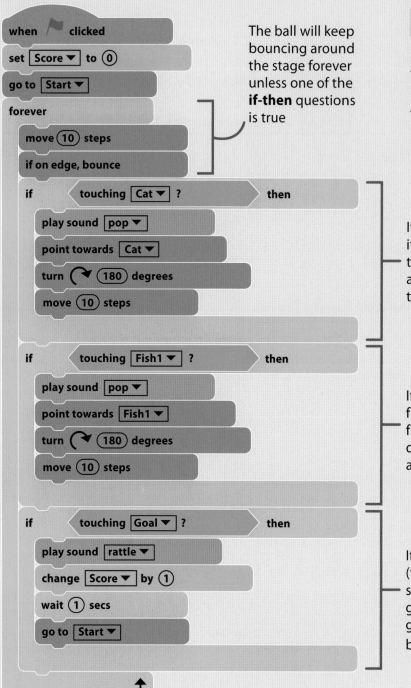

when 🚩 clicked
set Score ▼ to 0
go to Start ▼
forever
move 10 steps
if on edge, bounce
if touching Cat ▼ ? then
play sound pop ▼
point towards Cat ▼
turn ↻ 180 degrees
move 10 steps
if touching Fish1 ▼ ? then
play sound pop ▼
point towards Fish1 ▼
turn ↻ 180 degrees
move 10 steps
if touching Goal ▼ ? then
play sound rattle ▼
change Score ▼ by 1
wait 1 secs
go to Start ▼

The ball will keep bouncing around the stage forever unless one of the **if-then** questions is true

If the ball touches the cat, it "bounces" off the cat. It turns around 180 degrees and then moves away from the cat

If the ball touches the fish, it "bounces" off the fish. It turns around 180 degrees and then moves away from the fish

If the ball touches the goal (the green circle), the rattle sound plays and the score goes up by 1. Then the ball goes back to the start (the black ✗)

23 The soccer ball's script is now complete. This is how it should look. Read the script through carefully. Run the script and check that it works as it should.

24 To make Fishball look like a soccer game, click the **Choose backdrop from library** button in the stage info area, at the bottom-left of the screen. Select "goal1," "goal2," or "playing field." Click **OK** to load your chosen backdrop.

Click here to go to backdrop library

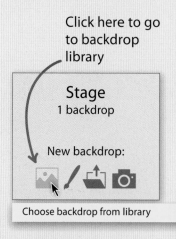

Stage
1 backdrop

New backdrop:

Choose backdrop from library

25 Good job—you've made your first Scratch game! Have fun playing it! The skills you've learned while making Fishball will help you to build the other games in this book—and even to invent your own games.

Show what you know
You've aced Fishball, but can you score with this quiz?

1. Label this map of the Scratch editor, using the key below the map. Write one letter for each of the colored sections.

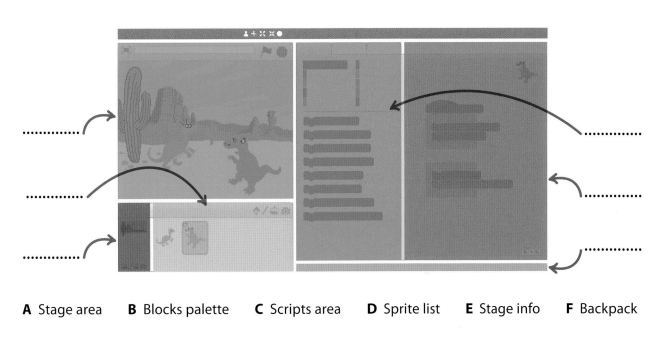

A Stage area   **B** Blocks palette   **C** Scripts area   **D** Sprite list   **E** Stage info   **F** Backpack

2. A .... repeats the blocks inside it nonstop.

3. An .... block either skips or runs the blocks inside it.

4. A .... is a block that stores data.

5. At the moment, the fish moves 4 steps at a time. Would these changes to the fish's **move** block make it swim faster or slower? Circle your answers.

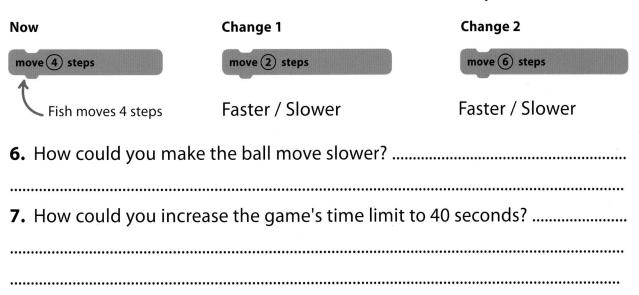

Now	Change 1	Change 2
move 4 steps	move 2 steps	move 6 steps
Fish moves 4 steps	Faster / Slower	Faster / Slower

6. How could you make the ball move slower? ....

....

7. How could you increase the game's time limit to 40 seconds? ....

....

....

Ghost Hunt

Things get spooky in this game! You're a witch on a broomstick flying around the city at night in search of friendly ghosts. Ghost Hunt will put your keyboard skills to the test!

What you'll learn:
• How to use keyboard controls to move a sprite
• How coordinates can tell sprites where to go
• That Scratch can use random choices to make games unpredictable

The score and time left in the game are shown here

The ghost glides eerily across the screen

Use the green flag and red button to start and stop the game

Ghost Hunt
by HappyShrimp123 (unshared)

Score 9

Time 5

You can move the witch anywhere on the screen using the arrow keys on the keyboard

▲ Playing the game

Use the arrow keys to make the witch chase the ghost. When you touch the ghost, it disappears with a pop and you score a point. But the sneaky ghost can reappear anywhere, and it floats randomly around the stage! You have 30 seconds to score as many points as you can.

Good-bye Scratch Cat, hello witch!

The player's sprite for this game will be the witch. You won't need Scratch Cat on the stage, so it's best to delete him.

1 Start a new project. Click on the **File** menu and select **New**. Call the project "Ghost Hunt." As usual, you'll see Scratch Cat on the stage.

2 Go to the sprite list. Right-click on the cat with the computer mouse. Choose **delete** from the pop-up menu.

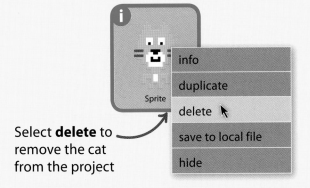

Select **delete** to remove the cat from the project

3 Click on the sprite symbol at the top of the sprite list to go to the library. Select the "Witch" sprite and click **OK** to load her into your game.

Click on the sprite symbol

New sprite:

Choose sprite from library

Witch

Coordinates

Scratch uses a pair of numbers called x–y coordinates to pinpoint a sprite's position on the stage. The x coordinate tells you where the sprite is across the stage, left or right. The y coordinate shows its up or down position. The coordinates will be positive for right and up, and negative for left and down. In Ghost Hunt, you'll use coordinates to send sprites to different parts of the stage.

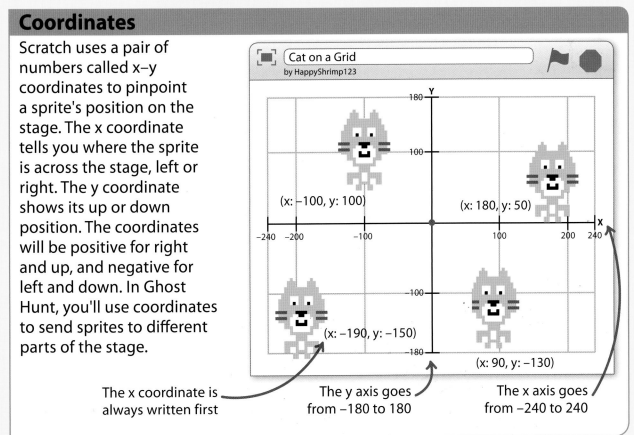

The x coordinate is always written first

The y axis goes from –180 to 180

The x axis goes from –240 to 240

4 With the witch sprite selected, build this script so that you can use the arrow keys to move her around the stage.

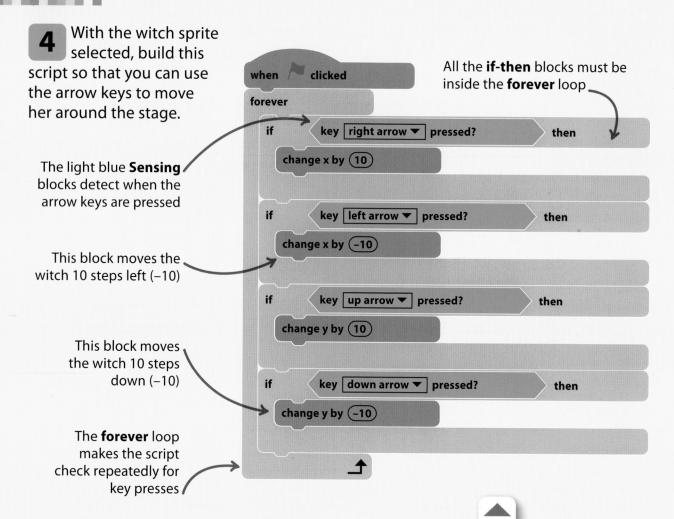

All the **if-then** blocks must be inside the **forever** loop

The light blue **Sensing** blocks detect when the arrow keys are pressed

This block moves the witch 10 steps left (–10)

This block moves the witch 10 steps down (–10)

The **forever** loop makes the script check repeatedly for key presses

5 Now run the project. You should be able to move the witch all over the stage using the four arrow keys. If it doesn't work, check that you have all the correct blocks and that they are all in the right place.

When an arrow key is pressed, witch moves 10 steps in that direction

A ghost in the city

It's nearly time to introduce the friendly ghost and get it gliding around the stage. But first, add some scenery to make the game look good.

Click here to open the backdrop library

Click OK to load it into the project

6 Go to the stage info area and click on the first symbol (**Choose backdrop from library**). Select "night city" in the library and hit **OK** to load it into the project.

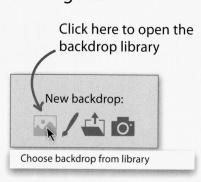

New backdrop:

Choose backdrop from library

night city
480x360

7 Click on the sprite symbol at the top of the sprite list to open the sprite library. Then select "Ghost1" and click **OK** to add it to your project.

Ghost1

8 Next, build the script shown below in Ghost1's script area. This script uses randomly chosen coordinates to make the ghost float unpredictably around the stage. Run the script.

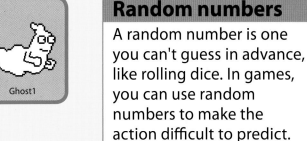

Random numbers

A random number is one you can't guess in advance, like rolling dice. In games, you can use random numbers to make the action difficult to predict.

Makes the ghost appear at the start of game

Scratch picks random coordinate numbers from within this range

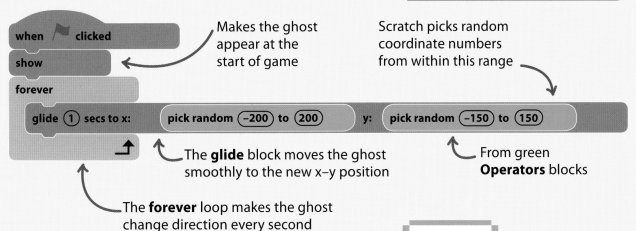

```
when [flag] clicked
show
forever
    glide (1) secs to x: (pick random (-200) to (200))  y: (pick random (-150) to (150))
```

The **glide** block moves the ghost smoothly to the new x–y position

From green **Operators** blocks

The **forever** loop makes the ghost change direction every second

Scoring, timing, and music

At the moment, you have two sprites and a nice backdrop. To turn this project into a game, you need to set up a scoring system and a time limit. Adding some music will help to make the game more fun.

Time's running out!

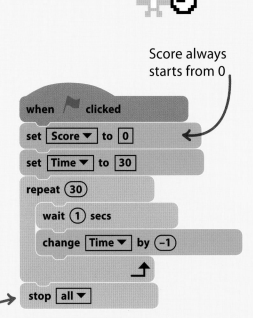

9 Select the witch, then go to the orange **Data** section. Create two new variables for all sprites and call them **"Score"** and **"Time."** Leave their boxes ticked so they show on the stage during the game.

10 Now add this script to the witch sprite. It sets the score to zero at the start of the game. Then it counts down the seconds from 30 and ends the game at 0.

After 30 seconds, this block ends the game

Score always starts from 0

```
when [flag] clicked
set [Score] to [0]
set [Time] to [30]
repeat (30)
    wait (1) secs
    change [Time] by (-1)

stop [all]
```

Script waits here until sprites collide

11 Make this extra script for the ghost. It adds a point to the score every time the witch touches the ghost. The ghost immediately vanishes with a pop, but then reappears somewhere else.

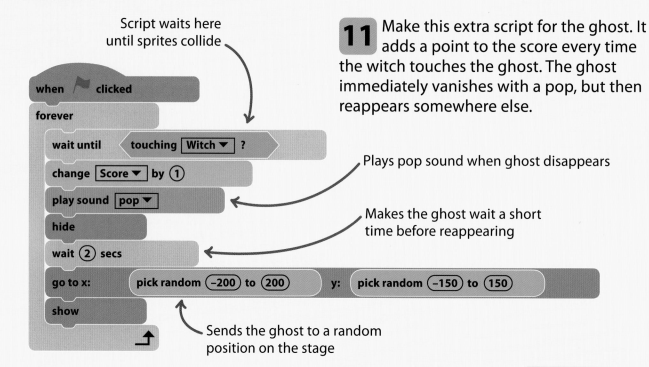

```
when  clicked
forever
    wait until       touching Witch ▼ ?
    change Score ▼ by 1
    play sound pop ▼
    hide
    wait 2 secs
    go to x:    pick random -200 to 200    y:    pick random -150 to 150
    show
```

Plays pop sound when ghost disappears

Makes the ghost wait a short time before reappearing

Sends the ghost to a random position on the stage

12 Run the game. You'll probably find that the sprites are so big that they bump into each other too easily, especially in the middle of the stage. To help fix this, add these two short scripts. The first is for the witch, the second is for the ghost.

```
when  clicked
go to x: 0 y: -140
set size to 50 %
```

Starts the witch at the bottom of the stage

Makes the witch sprite half her normal size

```
when  clicked
set size to 50 %
```

Reduces the ghost's size by half

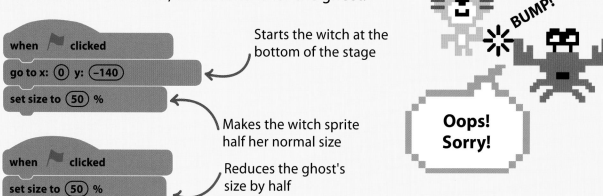

Ouch!

BUMP!

Oops! Sorry!

13 For the final touch, add some music. Select the witch sprite, go to the sound library, and load "dance magic." Then add this script to loop the music.

```
when  clicked
forever
    play sound dance magic ▼ until done
```

The music plays nonstop while the game runs

14 Run the game again. You should find that it's more of a challenge now. Play it with your friends—who can catch the most ghosts?

It's the witching hour!

Show what you know
You're a top ghost hunter, but do these brainteasers spook you?

1. Which order are coordinates written in, (x, y) or (y, x)? ....

2. What are the coordinates of the black x's on this picture of the stage?

A. (_____, _____)   **B.** (_____, _____)   **C.** (_____, _____)   **D.** (_____, _____)

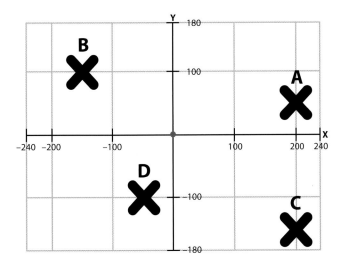

3. Add x's to the stage at these coordinates and label them a, b, c, and d:

a. (100, 0)

b. (0, 50)

c. (−100, −100)

d. (−200, −50)

4. In which direction do these blocks move a sprite: up, down, left, or right?

| change x by (100) | change y by (−150) | change y by (50) | change x by (−200) |

....

5. Circle the block that moves a sprite smoothly to a particular x–y position.

| go to x: (0) y: (0) | glide (1) secs to x: (0) y: (0) | change x by (10) |

6a. How would you make the ghost speed up? ....

....

6b. How would you slow down the witch? ....

....

7. Where would you put a **point in direction 90** block and **point in direction −90** block in the witch's main script to make her face the correct way when you press the right and left arrow keys? Try out your ideas.

Rapid Reaction

In this game, two players compete to see who has the fastest reaction time. Hit your key with lightning speed to win. If you hesitate for even a fraction of a second, you'll taste defeat!

What you'll learn:
• How to draw sprites and paint backdrops
• How to use the Scratch timer in games
• How to write game instructions and show them on the stage

Player 1's time is shown here

The green circle tells you which player has won

Player 2's time is shown here

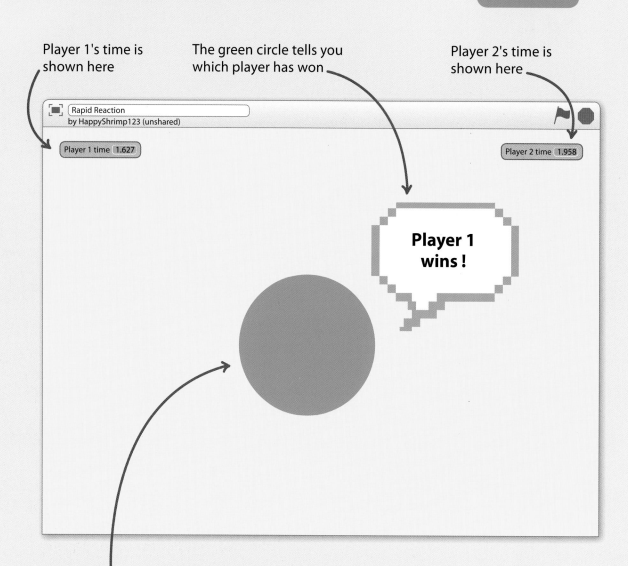

Rapid Reaction
Player 1 time 1.627

Player 2 time 1.958

Player 1 wins !

Rapid Reaction has only one sprite—a circle that turns from red to green

▲ Playing the game

Clicking the green flag shows the instructions on the stage. Each player has a different key to press: Player 1 the "Z" key, Player 2 the "M" key. When you're ready to play, hit the space bar. Wait until the red circle turns green, then whoever presses fastest wins the game.

Creating the big circle

There's only one sprite in this game. It's a simple colored circle that you can draw yourself using Scratch's paint editor. The circle starts off red, telling the players to wait before pressing. Then some Scratch magic turns it green to signal "Go!"

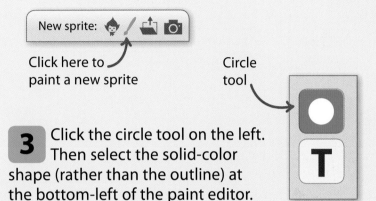

Red says "Wait!"

Green says "Go!"

1 Start a new project and name it "Rapid Reaction." Click the paintbrush symbol at the top of the sprite list to open the paint editor.

New sprite:

Click here to paint a new sprite

Circle tool

2 Check that **Bitmap Mode** is selected in the bottom-right corner of the paint editor. Then choose red on the color palette.

3 Click the circle tool on the left. Then select the solid-color shape (rather than the outline) at the bottom-left of the paint editor.

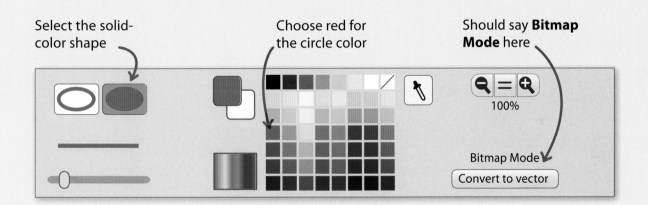

Select the solid-color shape

Choose red for the circle color

Should say **Bitmap Mode** here

100%

Bitmap Mode

Convert to vector

4 While holding down the shift key, click and drag with the mouse to draw a circle. The circle should be a little bigger than the cat. Click outside the circle. Look at the stage to compare your circle to the cat. When you're happy with the circle's size, drag it to the center of the stage. Then right-click on the cat and select delete.

See you later!

Resizing the circle

You can use the **Shrink** and **Grow** tools at the top of the Scratch screen to make your circle smaller or bigger. Click on the tool and then on the thing you want to shrink or grow.

Shrink

Grow

Scripts for the sprites

You'll build most of the code for Rapid Reaction in the scripts area of the circle sprite. This game uses Scratch's built-in timer. You can find blocks for the timer in the light blue **Sensing** section.

6 Add this script to the circle sprite. After hitting the space bar, it records how long Player 1 takes to hit the "Z" key. It also checks to see if Player 1 reacts first.

Pressing "Z" runs the rest of the script

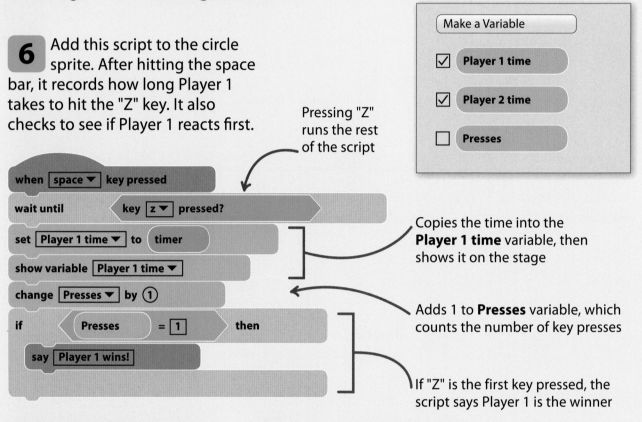

Copies the time into the **Player 1 time** variable, then shows it on the stage

Adds 1 to **Presses** variable, which counts the number of key presses

If "Z" is the first key pressed, the script says Player 1 is the winner

Comparison operators

In the **Operators** section are three green blocks that compare what's in their two windows. You can use a **comparison operator** in an **if-then** block to decide when the blocks inside it are run.

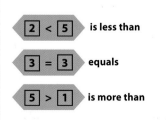

2 < 5   **is less than**

3 = 3   **equals**

5 > 1   **is more than**

5 In the **Data** section of the **Scripts** tab, make three variables for all sprites: **"Player 1 time," "Player 2 time,"** and **"Presses."** Uncheck the checkbox for **Presses.**

Make a Variable
☑ **Player 1 time**
☑ **Player 2 time**
☐ **Presses**

7 Now build the script below to record Player 2's reaction. It's almost the same as the last script, except that it's triggered by the "M" key and it uses the **Player 2 time** variable.

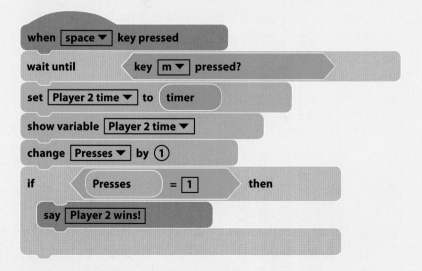

Script waits between 3 and 6 seconds after space key is pressed before changing the circle's color

8 This new script makes the red circle turn green to tell the players to press their keys. It lets the timer run until both players have pressed. If their reaction times are the same, it's a draw.

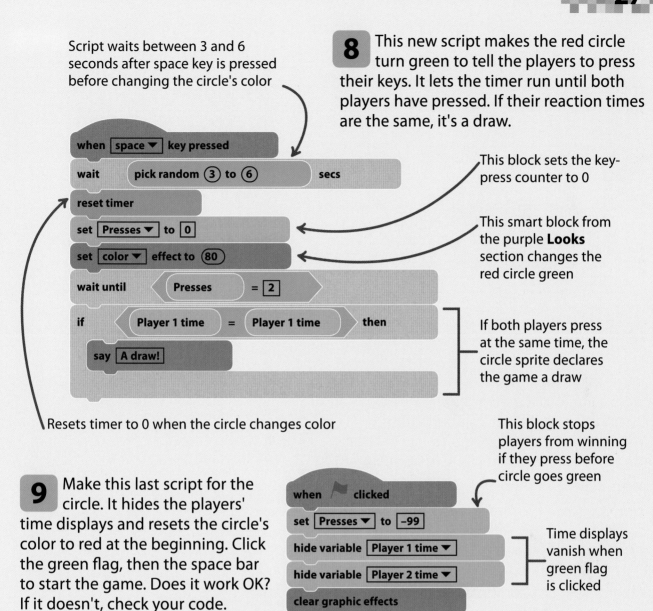

This block sets the key-press counter to 0

This smart block from the purple **Looks** section changes the red circle green

If both players press at the same time, the circle sprite declares the game a draw

Resets timer to 0 when the circle changes color

9 Make this last script for the circle. It hides the players' time displays and resets the circle's color to red at the beginning. Click the green flag, then the space bar to start the game. Does it work OK? If it doesn't, check your code.

This block stops players from winning if they press before circle goes green

Time displays vanish when green flag is clicked

Cancels the **set color effect to 80** block

Instructions

So that the players know the rules of Rapid Reaction, you can create a special sprite that shows the instructions when the game begins.

Click on the big **"T"**

How do I play this game?

10 Your instructions sprite will just be text on a see-through background. Use the paintbrush symbol to create a new blank sprite and call it "Instructions." Make sure you are in **Bitmap Mode** in the paint editor. Then select the text tool on the left.

11 Choose black from the palette as the color for the text. Click on the checkered drawing area and type out the instructions shown on the right.

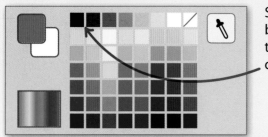

Select black for the text color

Who has the quickest reactions?

When circle goes green: Player 1 press Z Player 2 press M

Press space bar to start.

12 You can change the look of the type at this stage by clicking on **Font** at the bottom-left of the paint editor. There are six fonts to choose from. If the text doesn't fit, use the **Select** tool (the hand symbol) to resize it. Drag a box around the text and pull the corner points of the text box in or out. When you're finished, click outside the box to stop editing.

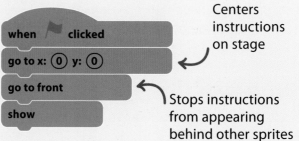

Who has the quickest reactions?

When circle goes green: Player 1 press Z Player 2 press M

Press space bar to start.

Select tool

Use the corner points to resize the block

13 Give the instructions sprite these scripts. They show the instructions at the start of the game, then hide them when the space bar is pressed. Run the game to check that the scripts work.

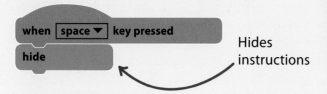

when [space ▼] key pressed
hide

Hides instructions

when 🏁 clicked
go to x: ⓪ y: ⓪
go to front
show

Centers instructions on stage

Stops instructions from appearing behind other sprites

14 Now go to the stage. Click on the **Player 2 time** window. Drag it into the top-right corner. This will help each player to see their time clearly.

Fill with color tool

15 Lastly, add a colored backdrop. To open the paint editor, click the paintbrush in the stage info area (bottom-left of the screen). Pick a color, select the **Fill with color** tool (the paint pot), and click on the drawing area. That's it—you're ready to play Rapid Reaction!

Paint new backdrop

New backdrop:

Show what you know
How will you react when you tackle these fiendish questions?

1. You can resize sprites using the .... and .... tools above the stage, at the top of the Scratch screen.

2. Which of these tools will you NOT find in the Scratch paint editor? Mark your answer.

● ....   T ....

(fill) ....   (scissors) ....

3. In which section will you find the **timer** block? ....

4. True or false: unchecking a variable's checkbox will make it appear on the stage. ....

5. Which coordinates center a sprite on the stage? Circle your answer.

go to x: (240) y: (180)   go to x: (100) y: (-180)   go to x: (0) y: (0)

6. Try putting these numbers into the window of the **set color effect to** block. What colors do you get when the red circle changes?

20 ....   30 ....   100 ....

130 ....   150 ....   180 ....

7. What do these three comparison operator blocks mean?

a > b   c < d   d = e

a .... b   c .... d   d .... e

8. To make the game more fun, you can add sounds that play when the players press their keys. Where would you put these two blocks in the players' scripts? Try out your ideas in Scratch.

Player 1   **Player 2**

play sound [duck ▼]   play sound [goose ▼]

Melon Bounce

Scratch Cat has to stop the falling watermelons from hitting the ground, but he doesn't know where they'll appear or which melon will drop first! Help him to keep the melons in the air.

What you'll learn:
• How to animate a sprite by making it quickly swap its costumes
• How to make copies of sprites and their scripts
• That time delays can make games more fun

Each melon starts in a random position

The melons bounce off the cat and back up into the air

The melons fall one by one

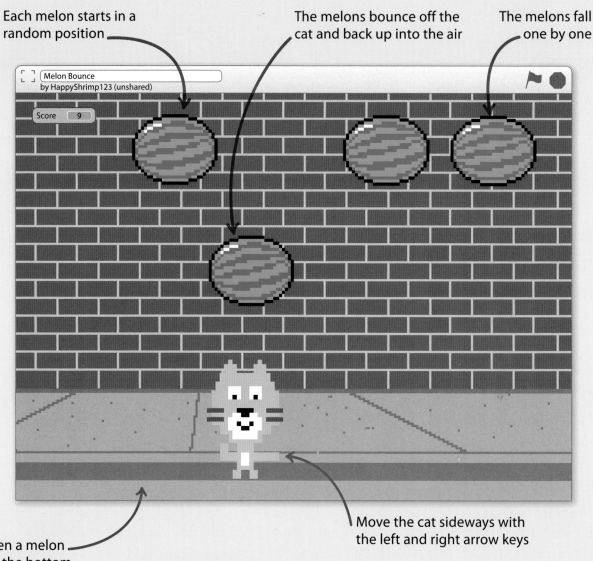

When a melon hits the bottom of the stage, you hear a cymbal and it's the end of the game

Move the cat sideways with the left and right arrow keys

▲ Playing the game

Use the arrow keys to move Scratch Cat back and forth across the stage to reach the falling melons. You get a point for every second the game lasts. The longer you keep the melons bouncing, the more points you score!

Getting the cat moving

First, make some code so that Scratch Cat can patrol along the bottom of the stage, keeping the watermelons off the ground.

1 Start a new project and name it "Melon Bounce." Change the cat's name from "Sprite1" to "Cat."

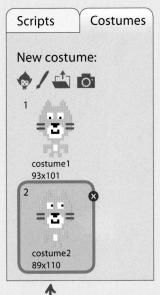

2 Look under the cat's **Costumes** tab. You'll see he has two costumes. If you make him switch costumes repeatedly, it will look like he is walking. This is called animation.

Quick costume changes make the cat appear to walk

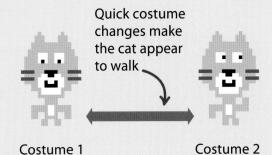

Costume 1 ⟷ Costume 2

Sprite's costumes are listed in order

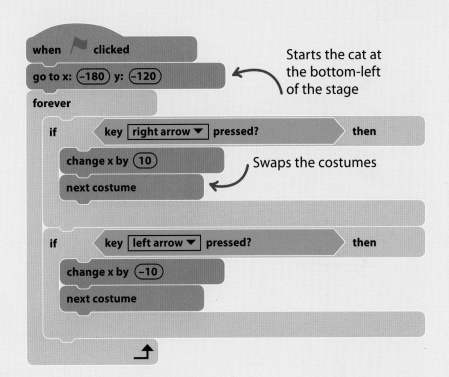

Starts the cat at the bottom-left of the stage

Swaps the costumes

3 Create this script so that you can move the cat along the bottom of the stage using the left and right arrow keys. The purple **next costume** blocks change the cat's costume every 10 steps.

Multiple melons

To make the four melons, you'll load one sprite, give it one script, and then make three copies of it.

4 In the sprite list, click on the sprite symbol (**Choose sprite from library**). Load the "Watermelon" sprite.

Watermelon

5 Add a sound for when the melon hits the ground. Under the watermelon's **Sounds** tab, click on the speaker symbol (**Choose sound from library**). Load the "cymbal" sound.

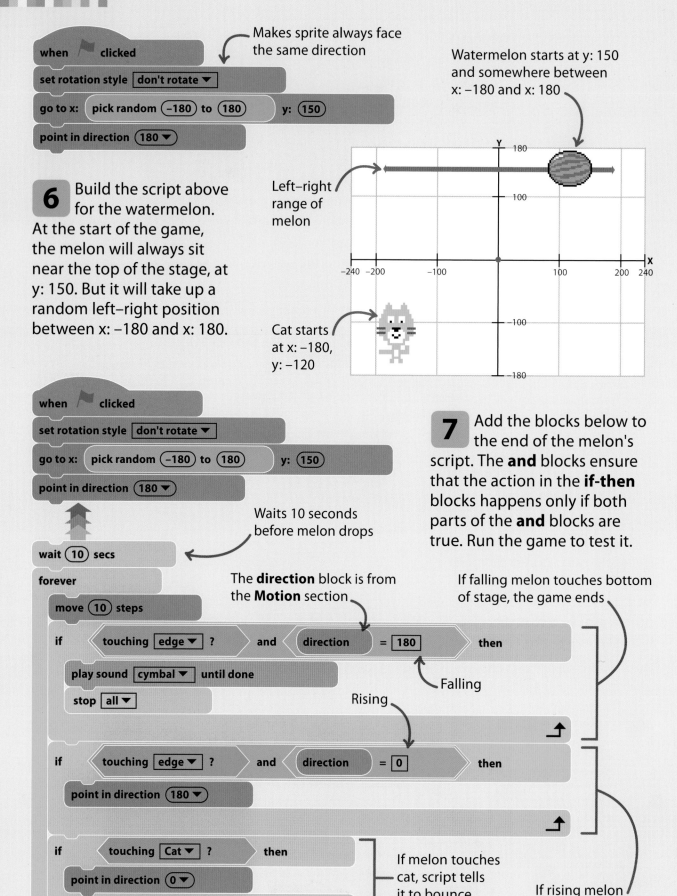

Makes sprite always face the same direction

```
when ⚑ clicked
set rotation style [don't rotate ▼]
go to x: (pick random (-180) to (180))  y: (150)
point in direction (180 ▼)
```

Watermelon starts at y: 150 and somewhere between x: –180 and x: 180

6 Build the script above for the watermelon. At the start of the game, the melon will always sit near the top of the stage, at y: 150. But it will take up a random left–right position between x: –180 and x: 180.

Left–right range of melon

Cat starts at x: –180, y: –120

```
when ⚑ clicked
set rotation style [don't rotate ▼]
go to x: (pick random (-180) to (180))  y: (150)
point in direction (180 ▼)
```

Waits 10 seconds before melon drops

7 Add the blocks below to the end of the melon's script. The **and** blocks ensure that the action in the **if-then** blocks happens only if both parts of the **and** blocks are true. Run the game to test it.

The **direction** block is from the **Motion** section

If falling melon touches bottom of stage, the game ends

```
wait (10) secs
forever
  move (10) steps
  if < touching [edge ▼] ? > and < (direction) = [180] > then
    play sound [cymbal ▼] until done
    stop [all ▼]
  if < touching [edge ▼] ? > and < (direction) = [0] > then
    point in direction (180 ▼)
  if < touching [Cat ▼] ? > then
    point in direction (0 ▼)
```

Falling

Rising

If melon touches cat, script tells it to bounce upward again

If rising melon touches top of stage, it drops back down

8 To make the game trickier, add three more melons. Copy the watermelon and its code by right-clicking on it and selecting **duplicate** from the pop-up menu. Do this two more times, so you have four melons.

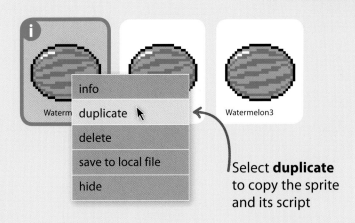

Select **duplicate** to copy the sprite and its script

9 Change the **wait 10 secs** block in the scripts of the three duplicate melons so that the melons all drop at different times. Alter their waiting times to 15, 20, and 25 seconds.

Watermelon2

go to x: pick random (−180) to

point in direction (180 ▼)

wait (15) secs

forever

Make this 15 seconds

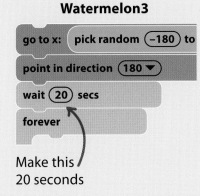

Watermelon3

go to x: pick random (−180) to

point in direction (180 ▼)

wait (20) secs

forever

Make this 20 seconds

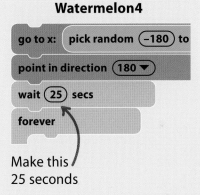

Watermelon4

go to x: pick random (−180) to

point in direction (180 ▼)

wait (25) secs

forever

Make this 25 seconds

Scoring and scenery

You've nearly finished building Melon Bounce. All that's left to do is to create a script to keep score and to add some scenery to the stage.

What a waste of melons!

10 Make a new variable for all sprites called **"Score."** Leave its checkbox checked. Add this script to the cat. It adds 1 to the score for every second that the game lasts.

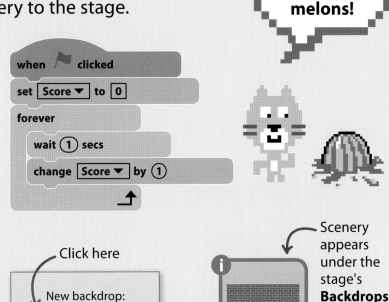

when ⚑ clicked

set [Score ▼] to [0]

forever

wait (1) secs

change [Score ▼] by (1)

11 Go to the stage info area and click on the first symbol (**Choose backdrop from library**). Select "brick wall1" in the library and hit **OK**. The game's now complete. Keep those melons in the air!

Click here

New backdrop:

Choose backdrop from library

Scenery appears under the stage's **Backdrops** tab

brick wall1 480x360

Show what you know

Now that you've mastered the melons, try these mind-bogglers.

1. What color are the blocks in these sections of the blocks palette?

Data ....

Sound ....

Events ....

Sensing ....

Motion ....

Control ....

Operators...

Looks...

2. Quickly switching a sprite's costumes to make it look as if it's walking or running is called ....

3. Would making the cat move faster make the game easier or harder?...

4. How could you make the melons fall faster? ....
....

5. How could you make the melons smaller?...
....

6. How could you add more melons to the game?...
....

7. The melons occasionally bunch together at the start, which makes the game far too easy. You can fix this by changing the **pick random** range in the **go to x** blocks of the melon's scripts, as shown below. Try it yourself.

Watermelon

pick random (40) to (180)

Watermelon2

pick random (40) to (180)

Watermelon3

pick random (-180) to (-40)

Watermelon4

pick random (-180) to (-40)

How does this solve the bunching problem? ....
....
....

8. Try building a short script to play music while the game is running. Add it to the cat sprite. Test your script.

Solutions

Good job, you've completed all the tasks! Time to check your "Show what you know" answers. How did you do? Are you a Scratch games master now?

We know all the answers!

pages 4–5 Meet Scratch

1. A character or object that can move or react is a **sprite**.
2. A **script** is a set of blocks joined together.
3. A **costume** is a picture that a sprite can show on the stage.
4. To run (start) a program, you click the **green flag**.
5. A **library** is a collection of sprites, sounds, or backdrops.
6. Scratch measures distances on the stage in units called **steps**.

pages 8–17 Fishball

1.

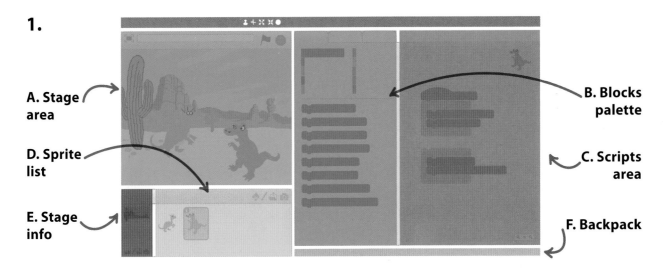

A. Stage area
D. Sprite list
E. Stage info
B. Blocks palette
C. Scripts area
F. Backpack

2. A **forever loop** repeats the blocks inside it nonstop.
3. An **if-then** block either skips or runs the blocks inside it.
4. A **variable** is a block that stores data.

5.

Change 1

move ② steps

Faster / Slower

Change 2

move ⑥ steps

Faster / Slower

6. To make the ball move slower, change the number in each of its three **move** blocks to less than 10. For example, if you type in 5, the ball will move at half the speed.

move ⑩ steps

Any number less than 10 will slow the ball down

7. To lengthen the game to 40 seconds, change both values of 30 in the timing script to 40. To make the game shorter, type in values less than 30.

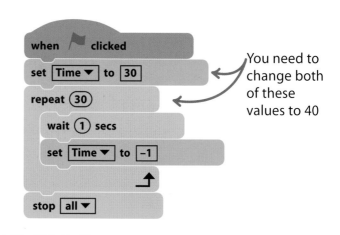

when ⚑ clicked
set [Time ▼] to [30]
repeat ③⓪
    wait ① secs
    set [Time ▼] to [−1]

stop [all ▼]

You need to change both of these values to 40

pages 18–23 Ghost Hunt

1. Coordinates are always written **(x, y)**.

2. A. (200, 50)   **B.** (−150, 100)   **C.** (200, −150)   **D.** (−50, −100)

3. The x's you drew should be in roughly the same positions as the red x's shown here.

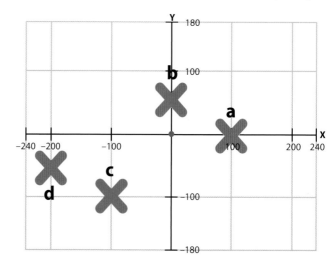

4.

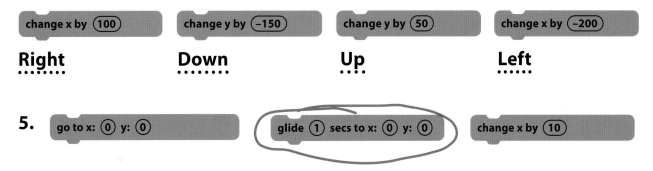

| change x by (100) | change y by (−150) | change y by (50) | change x by (−200) |

Right .... **Down** .... **Up** .... **Left** ......

5.

go to x: (0) y: (0)   glide (1) secs to x: (0) y: (0)   change x by (10)

6a. To speed up the ghost, reduce its glide time in the **glide** block.

glide (1) secs to x: [pick random (−200) to (200)] y: [pick random (−150) to (150)]

If you change this to 0.5 seconds,
the ghost will move twice as fast

6b. To slow down the witch, reduce the 10 and −10 steps in her **change x by** and **change y by** blocks to smaller values, such as 5 and −5.

7. Put the **point in direction 90** block in the witch's right arrow **if-then** block. The **point in direction −90** block goes in her left arrow **if-then** block.

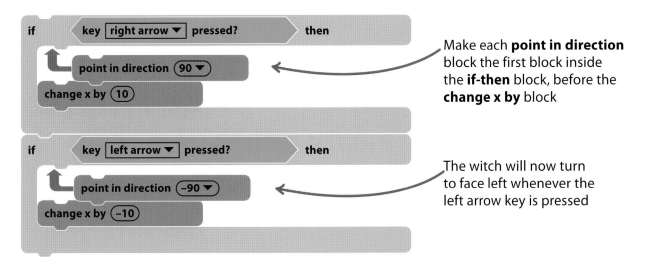

if [key [right arrow ▼] pressed?] then
    point in direction (90 ▼)
change x by (10)

Make each **point in direction** block the first block inside the **if-then** block, before the **change x by** block

if [key [left arrow ▼] pressed?] then
    point in direction (−90 ▼)
change x by (−10)

The witch will now turn to face left whenever the left arrow key is pressed

You'll notice that the poor witch now spends half her time upside down! To fix this, select her in the sprite list, click on the blue **(i)** and change her rotation style to left–right.

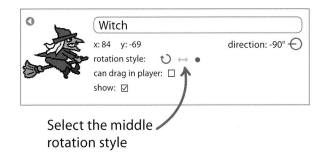

Witch
x: 84   y: -69   direction: -90°
rotation style: ↻ ↔ •
can drag in player: ☐
show: ☑

Select the middle rotation style

pages 24–29 Rapid Reaction

1. You can resize sprites using the **Grow** and **Shrink** tools above the stage, at the top of the screen.

2. The "scissors" symbol is the delete tool from the bar above the stage.

3. The **timer** block is found in the **Sensing** section of the blocks palette.

4. **False:** unchecking a variable's checkbox will *hide* the variable, not show it.

5. The coordinates **x:0, y:0** mark the dead center of the stage.

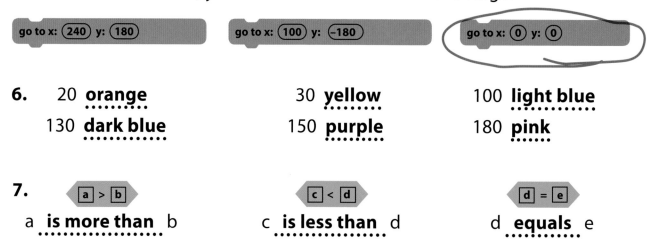

6.
20 **orange**   30 **yellow**   100 **light blue**

130 **dark blue**   150 **purple**   180 **pink**

7.

a **is more than** b   c **is less than** d   d **equals** e

8. Put the **play sound** blocks inside the players' **if-then** blocks. Don't forget you'll need to load these two sounds from the library if you want to add this code to your game.

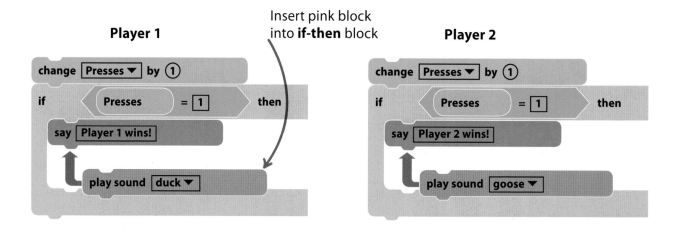

pages 30–34 Melon Bounce

1. **Data** blocks are **orange**
   Events blocks are **brown**
   Motion blocks are **dark blue**
   Operators blocks are **green**

   Sound blocks are **pink**
   Sensing blocks are **light blue**
   Control blocks are **yellow**
   Looks blocks are **purple**

2. Quickly switching a sprite's costumes to make it look as if it's walking or running is called **animation**.

3. Making the cat move faster would make the game **easier**.

4. You could make the melons fall faster by increasing the number of steps in their **move 10 steps** blocks.

5. You can make the melons smaller by clicking on them with the **Shrink** tool above the stage. You could also resize them by adding the purple **set size to** block at the start of their scripts. Type in the percentage you want them reduced by.

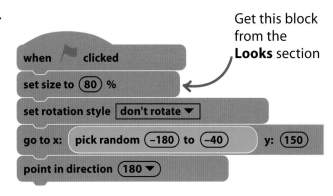

Get this block from the **Looks** section

6. To add extra melons to the game, select a melon in the sprite list. Then right-click and choose **duplicate** from the pop-up menu that appears.

7. The changes to the melons' **pick random** blocks make two melons keep to the left half of the stage while the other two keep to the right half. This stops all four melons from bunching up together.

8. You can base your music script on the one you built for the Ghost Hunt game. Choose any music you like from the sound library and load it into the cat sprite.

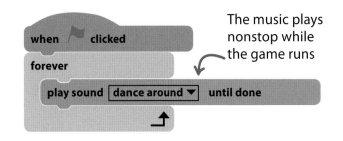

The music plays nonstop while the game runs

Getting Scratch

You can code online at the Scratch website, but if you aren't always connected to the Internet, you can install it on your computer.

I'm best— use me!

Scratch is easier to use with a mouse than a touchpad

Online Scratch

If you sign up for an account on the Scratch website, you'll be able to save your projects online and share them with friends.

1 Before you sign up to Scratch, get permission from a parent with an email address. Go to **scratch.mit.edu** and select **Join Scratch**. You'll need to set up a username and password. Don't use your real name as your username.

2 Once you've joined the Scratch website, click **Sign in** and then enter your username and password. Click **Create** at the top of the screen to start a new project. Happy coding!

Offline Scratch

When you don't have access to the Internet, or if you want to code offline, you'll need to download **Scratch 2.0** to your computer.

1 For the offline version of Scratch, go to **scratch.mit.edu/ scratch2download** and follow the installation instructions. The Scratch symbol will appear on your desktop.

2 To start Scratch, double-click on the **Scratch 2.0** symbol. When using Scratch offline, always save your work from time to time. (The online version saves automatically.)

Scratch 2

Note for Parents

The Scratch website is run by Massachusetts Institute of Technology (MIT). It is intended to be safe for children to use. The instructions in this book are for Scratch 2.0, not the older Scratch 1.4. The online version of Scratch works well on Windows, Mac, and Ubuntu computers; the offline version isn't compatible with all Ubuntu versions. At the time of writing, the Raspberry Pi can't run Scratch 2.0. Help your child work logically through any coding difficulties. Check for obvious errors, such as swapping similar blocks in scripts, and that scripts are controlling the correct sprites. Remember: coding should be fun!